Then *&* **Now**

KINGSTON-UPON-THAMES

Placing the Coronation Stone in its new site, 17 April 1935.

Then & Now

KINGSTON-UPON-THAMES

COMPILED BY CELIA MANNINGS

TEMPUS

First published 2001
Copyright ©Celia Mannings, 2001

Tempus Publishing Limited
The Mill, Brimscombe Port,
Stroud, Gloucestershire, GL5 2QG

ISBN 0 7524 2258 8

Typesetting and origination by
Tempus Publishing Limited
Printed in Great Britain by
Midway Colour Print, Wiltshire

The King George V Jubilee Fair, 1935.

Contents

Acknowledgements

I would like to sincerely thank the following people, who have helped me enormously during the compilation of this book:

My brother, Ian Harrison, the real writer of the family, who passed this photographic opportunity my way and was always on hand for advice; Jill Lamb, Margaret Kelly and Tim Everson for their time and efforts in the Local History Room, and for allowing me to use their photographic archives; my husband, Spencer, for continuing encouragement with all things photographic.

I would also like to thank the following for their time and helpfulness when taking photographs:

The Steadfast Sea Cadet Corps, in particular Mr Geoff Brown for his help and the photograph of the 1920 Sea Cadets; Sgt John McAree for his wonderful old police photograph; the Revd James Bates; Mr Paul Messeder and the Kingston Fire Brigade; Mr Richard Woodfin of St John's School; Mr Cook of Kingston Grammar School; Tiffin School; The Victoria Hospital; Celia Richings, Paediatric Outpatients, Kingston Hospital; Sue Hurlock of Kingston Library; Wilkinsons Store for allowing me on the roof.

Bibliography

Kingston Past	June Sampson
A Century of Kingston-upon-Thames	Tim Everson
Kingston, Surbiton and Malden in old photographs	Tim Everson
Kingston Then and Now	Margaret Bellars
The Book of Kingston	Shaan Butters
All Change Kingston, Surbiton and New Malden in the 19th Century	June Sampson

Introduction

In recent months I have been experiencing strange symptoms on heading into town. Everywhere I look I imagine horse-drawn carts, ladies in bodices and full-skirted dresses, medieval houses and punishments in the Market Place... Not the result of a new psychological syndrome, but of being asked by Tempus Publishing to write a book illustrating the changes occurring over the years in Kingston-upon-Thames. As a GP and mother of two young boys, this at first appeared an enormously daunting prospect, but my interest in photography has spurred me to the task. I have never trained in photographic technique and regard it as a hobby, but have found a fascination with history never previously realised, simply by standing with an old photograph in my hand and attempting to copy the scene some 100 years later. The most stunning are those in which the buildings and street layout are more or less the same but in which the people of Kingston, their dress, their vehicles, even their stance, are so unimaginably different from today.

On a personal note this has also been an achievement for me because, as part of an Army family, home is never the same place for much more than two years. Never before have I actually learned so much about, nor appreciated more, the insights into the town in which I live. This is to be recommended! When I started research having been here over a year, I admit to never having heard of, let alone seen, the Coronation Stone. It seems all too easy in the rigours of daily life to miss out on such a wealth of heritage and experiences. Kingston has had an Army presence for a great many years, and in a sense even as a temporary resident, this has given me a feeling of belonging.

Kingston undeniably has a wealth of history, and is the most fascinating of places to discover. My first task was to visit the Local History Room in Richmond Road and immerse myself in the archives of several thousand old photographs. One of the oldest known photographs of Kingston, for example, is of All Saints church, taken in 1866. Many books have been written about Kingston's history, and much research done, and it has been difficult, if not impossible, to find new information and unpublished photographs. I am therefore indebted to Kingston's local historians. This book, I hope, is different in that the aim has been to show each of the buildings and scenes as they are today, from exactly the same viewpoint where possible, or, if not, the buildings and scenes which have replaced them.

Most importantly the people of Kingston feature throughout the book. Kingston would not be the town it is today without nurses, firemen, police, shopkeepers, shoppers and more; the difficulty has been trying to include a picture from as many walks of life as possible in a limited space. The choice has inevitably been influenced by the available archival photographs; I would have liked to have included a market stall holder from one hundred years ago for example, but had no success in finding such a picture.

My second task was to take my camera and the old photographs into town and copy them. Not as easy as it sounds! One hundred years ago, there were not as many vehicles, nor did they travel as fast. Standing

Sailing barges unloading timber beneath Kingston Bridge, 1910.

in the middle of the road is not an option today. On being privileged enough to visit the roof of All Saints church tower, I was somewhat taken aback by the precarious route taken to get there; there are of course no modern staircases. The Grammar School kindly had no problem with me interrupting lessons, and the fire brigade squeezed in a photocall between emergency calls.

   With photographs prepared the remaining task was to write, I hope, informative and readable captions and assemble the whole into the final book. I have thoroughly enjoyed being able to experience Kingston's history along the way to doing this, and have been overwhelmed by how helpful everyone I have encountered has been. I hope that the final product does this, and Kingston, justice.

Celia Mannings
August 2001

In order to build the new Guildhall, and to make a platform for the Coronation Stone, Kingston's Hogsmill River needed to be contained within a culvert. The river then flowed through a concrete channel alongside the Guildhall, over which the platform was built. This can be seen in progress here in 1937, and was quite a feat of engineering. The Hogsmill flows from here under Clattern Bridge and onwards into the Thames.

In its new site next to the Guildhall, the famous stone can now be visited much more safely and is well out of the way of Kingston's ever-present traffic.

Clattern Bridge dates back to the twelfth century, and is one of the oldest road bridges in England. It carries High Street over the Hogsmill. At one time there was a cabmen's shelter close-by, where cab-drivers could rest and refresh their horses; the bridge was in fact originally called the 'Clattering Bridge' after the sound of the hooves which constantly crossed over the stones. This 1935 photograph is of the east side, showing the Victorian arches from one of many widenings. The photographer is standing close to where the Coronation Stone is today, now that its platform has been built. The arches on the west side are part of the original bridge, first documented in 1293, but thought to have been present as much as 100 years earlier. Today's photograph is taken from towards the edge of the platform in order to still see the bridge arches.

The Guildhall itself was opened in 1935 by Princess Alice, Countess of Athlone. It was designed by Maurice Webb, and cost £125,000. Building materials came from far and wide; the bricks from Oxshott, tiles from Cranleigh and the stone was Portland stone, while the timber came from around the Empire. Myrtle was transported from Tasmania, jarrah from Australia and pine from British Columbia.

Kingston had previously been governed for centuries from the old Market Place Guildhall, until the council expanded in 1891 necessitating a move to Clattern House, an eighteenth-century mansion to the south of the Market Place. This and neighbouring buildings were demolished in 1933 giving way to today's stunning building.

The River Hogsmill was central to early Kingston's economic life, flowing through the heart of town and supporting no fewer than five watermills there, as written in the Domesday Book of 1086. Kingston could almost have been known as 'Kingston-upon-Hogsmill'.

Upstream from the Guildhall was a well-known ford, called the Watersplash, which was not bridged until 1938. Here, at the turn of the century, horses and carts must progress through the water, while there is a footbridge for pedestrians. The Watersplash was on the corner of St James' Road and Penrhyn Road; now the area has been transformed by the construction of College Roundabout and a modern iron and concrete bridge takes the traffic over the Hogsmill.

Three of Kingston's watermills survived into the twentieth century. Chapel Mill, Middle Mill and Hog's Mill milled flour, linseed oil and even coconut fibre, at different times over the centuries. Chapel Mill became a candle factory after it was bought by William Smith in 1895, and the site is now a refuse depot. Middle Mill was sold to Kelly and Co. Printers and Publishers until they moved in 1932, after which the area was developed by Kingston University. The Coconut Pub in Mill Street and the Kelly Arms in Alfred Road are reminders of these early ways of life.

The most well-known owner of the Hog's Mill was John Marsh, who produced flour noted for quality and sold to the monarchy. The family took over the mill in the 1870s, already established as forage, hay and straw merchants. In 1896 it was sold to Johnston and Co., makers of Yewsabit metal polish, whose fame grew during the Boer War as suppliers of the British Army.

been Villiers Road since 1921. This delightful 1920 photograph shows a wonderfully idyllic rural scene where children play and paddle in the waters below the rickety timbers of the original bridge. In 1924 the wooden bridge was replaced by the Athelstan Bridge. It was the year of the Millenary of King Athelstan's Coronation, and on 5 November a window commemorating the event was unveiled in the Market House, as well as the opening of both the bridge and a new recreation ground in Villiers Road.

By 1997, however, the bridge became so weak that single file traffic was necessary, but now it has been strengthened and repaired along with a new traffic layout to help ease congestion.

Upstream a little further is Athelstan Bridge, carrying what was then Oil Mill Lane, over the Hogsmill. This road was named for the nearby mill which ground linseed, although it has

The River Thames has been the life-blood of Kingston for centuries. The town grew because of the river and then even more so because of the market. Charles I granted a charter in 1628 in which Kingston is described as 'a very ancient and populous town situated on the banks of the celebrated and navigable River Thames… from which town by means of that river, different goods and merchandizes, laden in wherries and boats, are daily transported backwards and forwards to our city of London and the adjacent parts'. This sums up Kingston's early days beautifully. Sailing barges are seen here around 1900, in front of Kingston's equally important bridge, the only one across the Thames upstream from London well into the eighteenth century.

Chapter 2

THE RIVER

Kingston's magnificent bridge began life as a rickety wooden one, albeit with strong and quality masonry foundations, possibly as early as the twelfth century. It was narrow, rotting in places and in constant need of repair. This picture of the old bridge is by Thomas Rowlandson, drawn around 1800. It was all to the good that an Act of 1825 allowed work to begin on a new bridge, fifty yards upstream. Designed by Edward Lapidge it took three years to build, and was opened by the Duchess of Clarence on 17 July 1828. Many buildings were demolished in order to re-route traffic onto the new approach road, which was named Clarence Street in honour of the Duchess.

This beautiful old photograph shows the view upstream from the bridge, with Kingston town centre to the left. The townspeople have always used the river to the full, and these photographs show how the buildings on the west side of the Market Place back onto the water. Part of the pagoda frontage of Nuthalls restaurant is still present today, once one of the most elegant social venues in Surrey, but closed in 1933, a victim of the Depression. A branch of Millets now occupies the site. The Sun Hotel's unrivalled gardens led down to the river, now Woolworth's. Today, however, a new venture is underway to build Charter Quay, with its 1,100 capacity 'Elizabeth Rose' style theatre

complex, apartments in Garricks House overlooking the river, a Piazza of restaurants and shops and a new riverside walkway.

FREE · FOR · EVER

butter, salmon, salt, arrows, coal, cloth and iron. Tolls were also payable at the time of the building of the new bridge, in order to pay for the building works and upkeep. When the tolls were lifted forty-two years later, there was great public rejoicing, as seen above in 1870.

Widening work has been going on for well over a year today, to the disappointment of modern-day drivers who regularly find themselves in lengthy queues of traffic on each side. The finished work, however, will be a great improvement. As yet there are no plans to reintroduce charges!

Tolls had come into being when a charter of 1448 by Edward VI, granted the right to charge fees on goods passing over the bridge for sale in the town. More than two dozen items were listed, among them wine, hogs, timber,

There are several old photographs showing Kingston's stretch of the River Thames completely frozen. This one is from as long ago as 1895 and shows the ice so thick that it supports the weight of adults. This could never happen today as the Thames has been kept too warm to freeze over since the building of a new power station in 1948. The Anglers Inn is on the extreme right, and the white-fronted building in the middle is Harris and Son Ironmongers. In the distance is the tower of the Native Guano Works, and the old electricity power station, just to the east of the bridge.

The Thames was vital to Kingston's economic growth. The town was a bustling inland port for centuries, being the main connection between London, Surrey and the surrounding counties. Principle buildings fronted onto the river, including factories, breweries, maltings, mills, boatyards, the tannery, and of course the wharves. Kingston's wharves were always busy; seacoal, timber, malt for the brewers, bark for the tanners, wheat for milling, and flour for distribution, were all constantly on the move. Palmer and sons shipped seacoal, working the wharves between 1869 and the 1960s. Gridley Miskin's timber barges, pictured here in 1948, sailed from Miskin's timber yard and stores often laden with giant tree-trunks from Surrey's ancient forests. Oak came via Kingston for the building of Westminster Palace, as did timber for the famous hammerbeam roof of Westminster Hall. Miskin's Wharfs occupied both the Middlesex bank and Thameside, between the road and railway bridges, and several of the sheds are present today on a preserved site.

Boat-building has long been an important trade. Excavations in 1986 revealed the site of a medieval boatyard on the Horsefair, with oak timbers from thirteenth-century cargo vessels. The Turk family are among the most well-known boat-builders, setting up business here and passing in succession from father to son to the present day. They have built boats for Queen Victoria, for the German Emperor, for the King of Belgium, racing craft used for the Thames regattas, and pleasure boats enjoyed in London's municipal parks. Jerome K. Jerome hired their rowing boats and his famous Three Men began their journey from Turk's boatyard, pictured here in 1930, on Thameside. Today Turks operate pleasure boats from moorings along the Portsmouth Road.

The Burgoines designed and built racing yachts and centre-board gigs until 1910. Other famous Kingston boat-builders were the Moulds, the Eastlands and W.H. Gaze and Son who produced more than 900 vessels for the Admiralty during the Second World War.

R aven's Ait, seen above around 1900, is an island in the Thames in Surbiton. It is thought to be that on which a treaty was signed in 1217 between the barons and Prince Louis of France, asking him to withdraw after the death of King John. For some unknown reason the island was known as Raven's Arse in the eighteenth century but it was changed to Raven's Ait in early Victorian times, becoming the home of regattas. Today it is privately owned and run, and is a centre for water sports as well as a venue to hire for special occasions such as weddings.

Kingston has always loved regattas, the river being important not only for prosperity but also for fun and sportsmanship. A Watermen's regatta began in the 1820s, with a 'Dogget's coat and badge' first prize. The first Kingston Amateur regatta was held on 1 July 1857 amidst downpours and thunder, organized from the Sun Hotel and viewed from its gardens. The following year the Kingston Rowing Club came into being with its headquarters on Raven's Ait, and in both 1864 and 1865 won the Grand Challenge Cup at Henley.

The Junior Kingston Rowing Club formed in 1869, organizing the first Thames regatta with fireworks and illuminated boats, helping to transform regattas countrywide into hugely popular public entertainment. This event became the annual Town Regatta, growing to include events such as naval battle re-enactments complete with gunfire. In 1900 the Kingston Borough Regatta was born, held for the first time on 30 July that year.

The old photograph shows just such an event, with Raven's Ait in the background. In contrast, the Marines are out in force in their Dragon boat, taking part in the Great River Race in the year 2000.

Kingston Rowing Club moved their headquarters to Canbury Gardens in 1955. Above is the idyllic scene northwards from Kingston in 1905, away from the wharves in the industrial town centre and looking towards the peaceful gardens and the bandstand, a place to enjoy the tranquillity of the river. The gardens were laid out in 1890-91, the bandstand being a gift from C.E. Nuthall, a former mayor. Almost 100 years later the riverside promenade is still a place to relax under the now mature trees. The Boaters Inn and the Rowing Club headquarters are just out of sight up ahead and a new bandstand replaced the old, which was removed in the 1950s. There are playgrounds and tennis courts in the gardens, and fairs and other events are often held in the summer months.

As the River Thames has long being a place for relaxation, so there have always been places to stay in Kingston. There had been a public house on the site of Anglers Hotel from as early as 1840, although the building in this 1910 photograph dates from a rebuild in 1901. The Anglers was a fashionable place to stay, situated on the riverfront at No. 61 Portsmouth Road, and boasted seven bedrooms, a bar and a dining room. This building was set back an additional eight feet from the road, to make it easier for traffic, such as the horse and carriage, (below) taking a breather, to pass around the corner. In 1958 the Anglers was demolished, and today the site is occupied by flats and offices, although the words 'The Anglers' (almost) remains on the end of the building.

P eople of all ages have always loved the river in Kingston. The Sea Cadets have flourished since 1911, when the unit was formed on board a brigantine called the *Steadfast*, moored alongside the Queen's Promenade to 'train local boys of good character in the ways of the Royal Navy and the Mercantile Marine'. In the 1920 photograph, the ship's company surround Chief Petty Officer Goodyear; some of the many hundreds of boys who have passed through their training over the century.

Sadly in 1928 the *Steadfast* succumbed to the corrosive effects of the Thames water, but the name continues as that of the Corps itself. A building was acquired from the Bentall family, which saw the unit grow from strength to strength to become one of the foremost units in the country. A brand new headquarters was completed in April 1998, and today both boys and girls train in rowing, sailing, shooting, seamanship, engineering and many more skills. Here some of the cadets prepare for a morning's training on the river.

The Market Place is the focal point of Kingston, and, other than the river, is the main reason for the town's existence. Today's bustling shopping centre can trace its origins back to the days of agriculture and farmland, and even now, despite the arrival of rail and road transport, the urban spread of London and decline in farming, the market has not only survived but flourishes. It is a pleasure to visit, as much to sit and revive with a cup of tea as to buy the weekly fruit and vegetables.

This photograph from the early 1900s shows that where there are now busy roads, crowded shops and housing, there were once open fields. Activities were more likely to centre around ploughing

and harvesting. This cornfield is now the environs of Ewell Road, an area built over with housing in the 1920s and '30s. Kingston and its market grew around the buying and selling of produce from vast areas of north Surrey, along with imports via the river, and still thrives today.

The earliest record of Kingston's Market is in the Cruria Regis Rolls of 1242, but it existed well before then. Royal charters give their backing and support. Charles I in 1628 granted 'that no other market shall from henceforth in future be created anew, or in any manner appointed, or in any way held in any place whatsoever within the distance of seven miles from the aforesaid town of Kingston-upon-Thames, either through us or anyone or any of our heirs or successors'. Historian John Leland wrote in 1525 'Kingston is the beste market towne of all southery'.

The seven mile privilege still applies today to the new borough boundaries, extended by Royal Charter in 1965.

Above is Kingston market day, a Saturday, in 1898. Today while vehicles and dress are dramatically different, many of the buildings remain unchanged. These days the market stalls are set up around and behind the Market House, leaving the square empty for events such as here during National Road Safety Week, or simply for chairs and tables from the cafés. The Charter Quay development is as yet under wraps on the left-hand side, where Hinde's emporium and other buildings once took pride of place.

The prominent feature of the Market Place is the Market House of today, the Guildhall of a century ago. It was designed by Charles Henman, and opened in 1840, replacing the original Guildhall built in the fifteenth century. From here, Kingston was governed by the borough council, after the Municipal Corporation Act of 1835 replaced the previous Court of Assembly.

In this 1902 photograph the then town hall is decorated to celebrate the Coronation of Edward VII. Today, although without decoration, the building itself is largely unchanged, other than by refurbishment. It was renamed the Market House when the council moved to Clattern House in 1891, and today can be hired for functions, or visited for refreshment in the café on the ground floor.

31

Queen Anne, sculpted by Francis Bird for £47 8s 6d, has gazed over her people going about their daily business in the Market Place since 1706. She graced both the original Guildhall and then the Market House, which has been her home since its opening. In 1902, Queen Anne's bicentenary year, the seven-times mayor of Kingston, William Finny, paid personally for repair and rebuilding. In 1993 when the Market House closed for a £650,000 refurbishment, Queen Anne was restored, over several months, by Plowden & Smith in Wandsworth. She was found to be filthy, with a broken wrist, a gown full of holes and a hollow body full of cement. She was, however, rejuvenated and re-gilded with gold leaf at a cost of £15,500 and has remained in her rightful place ever since.

Henry Shrubsole was a banker and mayor of Kingston three times over. In 1866 he and his brother John purchased the store which became famous as 'Shrubsole's, a store of the highest social standing', favoured by Queen Victoria and her family. In 1873 the store was bought by Joseph Hide and remained under this name until bought by House of Fraser in 1977. Today this building and others on the west side of the Market Place are being developed as Kingston's new Riverside Theatre Complex.

Henry Shrubsole, however, is remembered as a pioneer of the retail

shopping revolution, bringing people into Kingston rather than being lured into London. He was honoured by a memorial in the Market Place, a white marble statue of a woman and child, seen (left) in 1895. This drinking fountain was erected in his memory after he died suddenly while distributing tea to the elderly poor in 1880. Today it is regarded a little less reverently, and the steps are generally used for sitting on.

The photograph above shows the north-west corner of the Market Place in 1897, leading into Thames Street. The Olde Segar Shoppe on the right is one of Kingston's oldest buildings, dating back to the 1500s. Today it is part of Next. Rabbits and Sons the Bootmakers and Mangers the Drapers are on the left, long since rebuilt and transformed into Millets and Principles.

At one time there was a cattle market in the Market Place, until a sheep upset customers by wandering about in Boots the Chemists in 1925. It was then transferred to the Fairfield, although after the Second World War little farmland remained and it was no longer viable.

The Market Place is seen below from the south, on a Saturday in May, 1900. The horse bus is crowded with market visitors heading south into the High Street, and the joyous decorations are to celebrate the relief of the Siege of Mafeking in South Africa. The Griffin public house is on the left. Today, over 100 years later, many buildings remain but in a totally modern scene; it is hard to imagine the old one existed.

Before the twentieth century, general trading took place on Wednesdays, Thursdays and Saturdays, with the stalls dismantled after use to allow space for festivities, proclamations and even punishments; luckily the latter are not a feature today. Now the market operates six days a week, largely for produce, with a crowded general market on the Fairfield site on a Monday.

Harrow Passage is a narrow alleyway leading through into the Apple Market from the Market Place. These views are taken from the Apple Market end. In 1897, The Old Harrow Public House was on the left, but it became a shop in 1925 and is currently a bakers. The alleyway, however, retains its name. The building on the right is now the back of the premises of Laura Ashley's.

One of the iron pillars manufactured by Harris and Son, featuring the three salmon of Kingston's coat-of-arms, is still present, just. Today Harrow Passage is a busy little street, well-used by hurrying shoppers as a cut-through from the Market Place.

These views are of the Apple Market itself, taken from Eden Street, in 1896 and the present day. The changes are dramatic. Over the years there were indeed market stalls, in the 1950s with beautiful little tiled roofs, but today these have given way to shiny modern street furniture. Shops have come and gone. Thorntons Chocolates once occupied the foreground building on the left but now have branches in Clarence Street and Church Street. One sign of the times is the very modern lottery crossed fingers on the newsagent on the right.

High Street to No. 11 Market Place was a residential inn or hotel. One of the grandest was the Sun Hotel, famous for its 160ft long river frontage and landing stage, with beautiful riverside gardens, the perfect place to start the Kingston to Oxford pleasure steamers, and at one time headquarters for the Kingston Amateur Regatta. The Sun had twenty bedrooms and an excellent reputation. It took pride of place on the west side of the Market Place next door to the Joseph Hinde emporium, until bought by Woolworth's in 1930. With its transformation into one of the foremost stores in the chain, five centuries of history ended, there now being no inn in the Market Place at all.

Modern Kingston has no hotel in its centre, which is unusual in that at one time every building from No. 2

The Kingston Church Pageant was an annual event, here in 1921, drawing parishioners together and involving them in more than simply worship. The pageant play was performed as a series of tableaux, and afterwards each group posed for a photograph. This is Episode One, entitled 'Mythical'. Usually old Father Thames was a character in the story, but here there are Celtic maids bedecked with flowers, fierce warriors and many hooded Druids.

Chapter 4

PLACES OF WORSHIP

All Saints church is situated in the heart of Kingston, and has been central to worshipping Christians here for over a thousand years. The earliest church here was present in 838, when King Egbert of Wessex held an Ecclesiastical Council, a gift of land being made 'before the altar'. King Ethelred II was led here by the bishops at his Coronation in 979. All Saints may have been a Minster, dedicated to All Hallows, before it was destroyed by the Danes in 1019. They plundered and burned towns along the Thames leaving only bare walls standing; these old nave walls were incorporated into Kingston's first cruciform church, when Gilbert the Norman rebuilt All Saints in 1130. The tower was built on arches over the previous Saxon church.

This view is from Church Street, around the turn of the century. The buildings have changed little, although the shop selling underclothing and baby-linen is now Thorntons Chocolates. The ice-cream van is a regular presence in an otherwise ancient looking scene.

All Saints church overlooks Kingston Market Place and the Guildhall to the south, the river and bridge to the west, and the Clarence Street junction with Wood Street to the north, where the façades of John Lewis and Bentalls stores face each other grandly. This view is from a photograph by G.T. Jones and Co., in 1890, from the top of All Saints tower. The south-facing church gates are in the foreground, opening into the Market Place, where the old Guildhall dominates the centre of the picture.

Today, at 2.00 p.m. on a December afternoon, stall and street lighting is switched on. The new Guildhall can now be seen in the background, and the building of Kingston's new theatre complex is underway behind wraps to the right.

These views look to the west from the tower, showing the bridge and the Middlesex bank, in particular Gridley Miskin's on the right on the far bank. The buildings to the right on the near bank have disappeared under John Lewis's.

The tower itself from which these photographs were taken has a colourful history. In the fourteenth century it had a tall wooden spire, which was destroyed in 'a great weathering of wind, hayle, snow, rayne and thunders with lightening' in 1445. A valiant attempt at rebuilding was made in 1905 only for the tower to meet a similar end after 'the great winde and hurricane' of 1703. Strengthening and rebuilding

took place in 1708 and again in 1973 leaving the tower as it is today, although the thirteenth-century lower section survives.

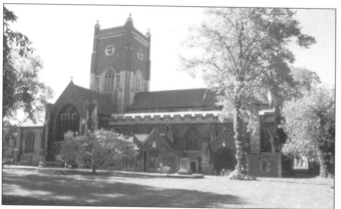

troops used the church as a stable, smashing tablets, monuments and pews. In 1699 6d in the pound was levied from parishioners to pay for repairs, and much alteration has continued since, especially in the nineteenth century. Today a £2.5 million appeal hopes to raise funds for much-needed restoration in order to prevent this Grade I listed building, the only one in Kingston, from closing. Roof, stonework and again tower repairs are all needed before installation of toilets and running water is undertaken .

These views are from Clarence Street, in 1905 and today. The graveyard was full by the 1830s and now burials take place at Bonner Hill Road Cemetery. The gravestones have been moved to the sides of the church grounds and the area landscaped.

The church has endured much during its long history, not only from the weather. Edward VI ordered that all items of value in England's churches be seized for 'the king's use', and all vestments and treasures were taken. In the Civil Wars, Roundhead

Esther Hammerton is one of the more famous old Kingstonians. Disaster struck in 1730 when she, her father and two colleagues were grave-digging by the small chapel of St Mary on the south side of the church. Her father, Abram Hammerton, who was sexton at the time, was killed when their digging disturbed the foundations and part of the chapel collapsed. Esther was rescued but sustained injuries which prevented her from wearing corsets. She succeeded her father as sexton, and apparently ever afterwards wore only

men's clothes. Excavations in 1926 revealed the site and it is now a permanent memorial.

The present day vicar, the Revd James Bates, would love to see the appeal succeed in order that All Saints can continue its days of service to the people of Kingston.

J. Dutter Pinx.   Jno. McArdell Fecit.

Est. Hammerton

~ Late Sexton of Kingston upon Thames ~

N.B. She was miraculously preserv'd under the Ruins of the Church which fell down as she was digging a Grave there, in the Year 1730. And notwithstanding she lay cover'd 7 Hours yet she surviv'd the Misfortune 15 Years.

Esther Hammerton was born 1711, died 1746. At the accident above related her father, who was sexton, and two other people were killed, and she received a hurt which prevented her from ever wearing stays. In consequence of this and of her occupation in her father's position, she ever afterwards used men's garments.

All Saint's reign as the only parish church in Kingston came to an end in 1942, when St Peter's church in Norbiton opened. The population at this time was ever-expanding and needs could not be met by one church alone. Today there are as many as fourteen parish churches in the Kingston deanery.

St Peter's flourishes today despite modernisation taking place around it. The old photograph is a delightful, gently scenic one whereas today new buildings in the form of retail space and six new flats are being built on the corner of Cambridge Road and London Road. This has for some time been the site of a boarded up LJ's. A new Boots store has also opened to the left.

This is St Luke's church in Gibbon Road, North Kingston, pictured in 1910 and largely unchanged today. It was built between 1888-1891 to serve the ever-increasing population of North Kingston following the coming of the railways in the second half of the nineteenth century. Farmlands and orchards around Canbury have become the densely populated area of Richmond Road. Lady Wolverton paid £1,000 for the spire to be built to make the church more visible, as she had failed to find it on her first visit.

Dr Edmund Staunton became vicar of Kingston in 1631 and remained so for twenty years until his expulsion for nonconformity. He had, however, instilled his beliefs in Presbyterian doctrines in his clerical assistant Richard Mayo, who began preaching to a group of parish 'rebels'. They met secretly in each other's houses until the Act of Indulgence in 1672 allowed nonconformists to meet openly, which they then did in a meeting house in Brick Lane. After the death of Mayo's son Daniel in 1733 disagreements arose and the group split. Those who remained founded the Baptist church in Brick Lane, now Union Street. The present Baptist church, seen above in 1902, was built in 1864. It is next to the old night watchman's shelter, which at this time was serving as the town mortuary. Today it is Bonbon Patisserie, a specialist cake shop, adjacent to the Garden of Remembrance.

Frank and his son Leonard continued the gradual expansion that made Bentalls the largest privately owned store in Europe until 1946 when it became public. This is the store in 1935 at the junction of Clarence Street and Wood Street, just before its demolition and the creation of the Hampton Court façade. In 1987 Bentalls teamed with Norwich Union to develop the Bentall Centre; the premises were demolished and replaced by a new department store linked to a four-floor shopping mall. The only surviving part of the old store is the Wood Street frontage, modelled by architect Aston Webb on the William and Mary Wing of Hampton Court Palace.

Clarence Street, Kingston-on-Thames

Clarence Street was once as pretty as a picture postcard, as in this 1910 scene from a postcard sent to Philadelphia following a day at the Kingston Regatta. This view is looking east away from the bridge. Kingston's main shopping street, Clarence Street, was originally London Road, but was renamed in honour of the Duchess of Clarence in 1828 when she opened the new Kingston Bridge. Bentalls store is on the left, advertising its fifty separate departments, now the entrance to the Bentall Centre. One chimney and gable-end are still present as can be seen in the distance on the right, but all the other buildings have changed. There are no vehicles now as Clarence Street has been pedestrianized, although the hot dog vendor is a regular feature.

These views show Clarence Street looking in the opposite direction, westwards towards the river, past the junction with Eden Street where the truck is turning in the 1952 scene. They are both taken from the roof of what was the Elite cinema and is now Wilkinsons store. Beyond the Eden Street turning, Clarence Street was then a two-way thoroughfare renowned for its congestion. Trolley buses were still in operation and remained so until 1961; a year later the traffic problems were eased by this part of the street being made one-way in the direction of the bridge. Finally, in July 1989, this part was pedestrianized. At the same time a new road system was constructed through the town in which the Kingston end of Richmond Road

became an extension of Clarence Street taking traffic one way round into Wood Street then on into Horsefair and across the bridge.

basement parking, and the reinforcement needed for building work so close to the Thames was tremendous. Some streets, like Old Bridge Street, sadly disappeared altogether under the modern buildings. Here (above) it is in August 1896, when it was the approach road to Kingston's first wooden Thames bridge. The pub on the right is the Black Lion, and Gridley Miskin's timber yard is in the background backing onto the river. Miskin's also had wharves on the opposite bank.

Today's photograph is from the junction of Wood Street and the Horsefair, behind John Lewis's, showing how the Horsefair runs straight through the building on its approach to the bridge. Behind the right-hand traffic lights the domed tops of what were Miskin's wharves can just be seen on the far side of the river.

Many buildings were demolished in order to make way for the John Lewis complex, another huge development undertaken at the same time as Bentalls. The award-winning design had to allow for the Horsefair to run through the site. Massive excavation work was carried out to allow for

Above is the Rose and Crown in Old Bridge Street, in 1896. At one time in Kingston there were as many public houses as one for every fifty residents in some areas, while ale was consumed at a rate of a gallon a day per head. Many of these old pubs have also been lost as a result of development, and the site of the Rose and Crown is also covered by John Lewis's. A medieval undercroft was discovered here during the building work in 1985, which was excavated intact. This cellar, together with the original bridge foundations, is currently in the basement of John Lewis's awaiting re-display to the public. The main entrance to the store is seen here on

the corner of Wood Street and Clarence Street in all its modern day glory.

Eden Street, originally Heathen Street, existed as early as 1315, when there were two shops, and formed the natural boundary of the town. The 'heathens' were probably country folk living in the fields and marshes around Kingston centre. Excavations in 1977 during the building of the Eden Street Shopping Centre showed that a branch of the

Thames once flowed through what is now Eden Walk, a clue to central Kingston's origins as a series of gravel islands, bounded and protected by the Hogsmill, the Thames, and this old Thames channel. Slow silting left marshy areas, even until recent times, dictating the siting of roads and buildings, hence Eden Street's characteristic bend towards the river, beginning in the distance in these photographs.

The 1904 photograph bears very little resemblance to that of today, most noticeably in that the Wesleyan Methodist church, opened in June 1890, has been demolished. Two years after its demise in 1964, a replacement was built in Fairfields South. Today Eden Street is a busy thoroughfare, seen here from its junction with Clarence Street which continues to the right where it has been pedestrianized.

Fife Road has been a busy shopping street for many years. This is Bryant and Noakes the 'economical tailors, outfitters and breeches makers', pictured in 1912. They opened at No. 21 Fife Road in 1909 and expanded to No. 23 the following year, sadly closing in 1967 after a long and distinguished career. More recently the site has been occupied by the Job Centre and then Escom Office Equipment.

Today the buildings are the home of the Kingston YMCA Shop, and are somewhat less picturesque after some severe modernisation. There was a YMCA in Kingston, opened by the Attorney General Sir Thomas Inskip on 18 April 1928, in Eden Street, but it closed in 1969.

its demolition in 1988.

The Elite Cinema, a 1,500-seat cinema built in 1921 at the east end of Clarence Street, was supposedly one of the most beautiful ever built. In 1946 it was bought by Granada who renamed it the Century. This caused a furore of local complaints including from the police who used the Elite as a landmark, so on 11 June 1951 it was renamed the Century-Elite, to everyone's satisfaction. This photograph was taken shortly before its demolition in 1955, when C&A took over until 1998. Wilkinson's general store now occupies the site.

To the right in today's photograph is Kingston's modern telephone box sculpture at the bottom of London Road, which has caused much debate over the years. The advertisement for Farebrothers Interment and Cremation Company is till on the wall above it.

Kingston has a place in cinema history as the home of Edweard Muybridge, the photographer who pioneered moving pictures. His birthplace was by coincidence next door to the first Odeon Cinema, launched in 1933 by Oscar Deutsch. The Odeon closed in 1967, and was then a bingo club until

The Empire Theatre was built in Richmond Road in 1910, and proudly boasted an illuminated dome, only the second after the London Coliseum. It opened on 24 October that year in front of the deputy mayor, Alderman Finny. It showed largely variety to an audience of up to 2,000 a night but closed on 27 March 1955 with the coming of television, the fate of many theatres at that time.

In 1997 the King's Tun public house opened on the site but the word Empire can still be seen in the brickwork at the side. Today, this part of what was Richmond Road is now a continuation of Clarence Street. The building work on the right is to be the site of the Rotunda, Kingston's new fourteen- screen Odeon cinema, complete with leisure centre, bowling alley and thirty thousand square feet of shops, restaurants and bars.

A famous landmark until 1965 was Kingston's last surviving Malthouse, at the top of High Street, seen here in 1906 with its distinctive kiln top. At one time there were breweries galore in Kingston, and the challenge was to walk down any street having a drink in each pub, and be sober at the end. Few could achieve it! The Old Malthouse dated from the early seventeenth century and was owned by Hodgson's Bewery until 1895, when it was bought by William Smelt and converted into an antique furniture shop. For seventy years its characterful appearance graced High Street, but only six weeks after it was given a preservation order there was outrage when it was illegally demolished.

Today, in a modern high street, a large office block stands on the site, and a white van has replaced the horse-drawn cart of ale.

The East Surrey Regiment were Kingston's local soldiers until 1959. Here, they are on parade outside the public library to mark the occasion of the unveiling of the memorial window, on 23 June 1905. The Boer War of South Africa (1899-1902), had at that time been the most costly to the people of Kingston, leaving thirty-three local soldiers dead, the majority from enteric fever. They were commemorated in 1903 by a plaque; both this and the memorial window are on display today in the library.

Chapter 6
PROTECTORS AND CARERS

The Keep is an impressive Victorian landmark on Kings Road, North Kingston, once the entrance to the East Surrey Regimental Barracks, seen here in 1910. Between 1875 and 1956 thousands of young men trained to be soldiers here; eighty-four thousand voluntary recruits in the First World War alone. Today the towers, battlements and magnificent arched gateway remain as a listed building at the entrance to what are now redeveloped married quarters for the present day Army, built in the 1970s. The name 'East Surreys' no longer exists as they merged with the Queens Royal Surrey Regiment in 1959 and then the Royal Hampshires in 1992, but in Kingston they will never be forgotten. The modern photograph, from November, shows a Poppy Day wreath hanging by the gateway.

In the First World War 6,000 officers and men were killed, and 1,196 died in the Second. The Holy Trinity chapel in All Saints church is dedicated to their memory. Here, the colours of the regiment are laid up in a commemorative service at the church on 29 September 1924. In 1944 the regiment received the 'Freedom of the Borough', allowing marching in the town 'with bayonets fixed, colours flying and drums beating'. This indeed took place in 1948 at the opening of the Kingston Power Station by George VI, and in 1952 at the regiment's 250th anniversary.

Today, families are important in military life; here my Army husband finds time to play with our sons in nearby Richmond Park.

IN CASE OF FIRE
Ass.t Foreman DEAN

In the early 1800s Kingston's fire-fighting equipment consisted of little more than a water container on wheels. There were no firemen and no alarms; when fire broke out, as it often did in the wooden buildings of Old Kingston, passers-by had to be encouraged usually with promises of beer, to lend a hand.

In 1870 a volunteer service set up headquarters in London Road, and used donations to buy one of the first ever horse-drawn fire engines, capable of delivering 350 gallons of water a minute. In 1887 they became the Kingston, Surbiton and District Fire Brigade, and opened a new station at No. 23 London Road. This delightful 1900 scene shows some of its proud members, still some years before the advent of the motor engine.

The fire-fighters and equipment of today have changed out of all recognition.

In 1908, Alderman Hall, the chairman of the Fire Brigade sub-committee, suggested the purchase of a new petrol-driven internal combustion engine. Finally on 14 January 1910, despite initial opposition from the council, the first motor engine was delivered, attracting crowds to view such a pioneering fire-fighting wonder. Water facilities had improved to a round-the-clock supply to the whole town, and when the second motor engine arrived some months later, the London Road station was too small. The engines are seen below in 1926.

A proposal was made to open a new station in Richmond Road complete with lodgings for the firemen, which would have cost only 30s a week, but this was turned down by one council vote.

Instead, London Road served until 1941 when a large depot set up on the Fairfield. Now, however, Kingston's modern station is in fact in Richmond Road, but cost rather more in 1959 at £46,000!

the Watchhouse, now a specialist bakers next to the Baptist church in Union Street.

In 1839 Kingston was made part of the Metropolitan Police district and a new police station was built in London Road in 1864, seen here in 1966. When it closed in 1968 it was found that there was no key to the front door as the building had been continuously open for 104 years. It is now the borough traffic wardens' office. The current police station is an imposing building next door to the Guildhall.

Attempts to control crime in medieval Kingston at first consisted of householders taking turns to watch at night. A watch had a constable, eight men and a beadle, who kept a fire and candle burning in the watchhouse. In 1773 Parliament passed an Act for the lighting and watching of Kingston, by which time 'every vice and every species of immorality was practised more or less openly'. But the 'Old Charlies' proved ineffectual, and in 1835 a Borough Police Act brought about a Watch Committee run along the lines of the Metropolitan Police. Constables appeared in uniform, armed with 'cutlass, rattle and staff', who collected lanterns and weapons each night from

Several of Kingston's police force, recognisable by the 'V' on their collars, are seen below in the late 1940s outside Kingston Police Station. They are checking equipment prior to handing over from an earlier shift to a late shift.

The modern patrol car, in contrast, is in Kingston's Market Place in April 2001 accompanied by the fire brigade and ambulances during National Road Safety Week. Demonstrations to the public took place reconstructing road traffic accident rescues, and advising on road safety. Sgt John McAree from the Kingston Traffic Division was on

hand with his colleagues to talk to passers-by.

within Kingston's workhouses for the poor. The first, in 1843, laid the foundations for today's Kingston hospital, but from the beginning it was too small; the second, designed by Charles Luck and completed in 1868, fared better with eighty beds in eight wards. In 1897, however, at a cost of £22,832, a new male infirmary was built, amazingly equipped for its time with 132 beds and a resident doctor. The hospital went from strength to strength especially during the First World War, and its name was changed in 1920 to Kingston and District Hospital.

The 1900 photograph is of the third workhouse infirmary, demolished in 1996. The modern structures of today have now replaced it, although the 1868 building still exists in use as offices. As can be seen, transport to hospital by ambulance is rather faster, today.

Kingston's first hospital stood in fields outside the town to contain the leprosy rife in medieval times. The second, the 'Pesthouse', was a successful isolation hospital, managing to stem the tide of the plague in 1593. After this, three infirmaries were built as a consequence of the number of sick

It was difficult in the 1800s to maintain nursing staff, as living conditions were poor, pay was low and work often dangerous. For example, an unfortunate workhouse nurse in 1840 cared for 'a pauper female in a paroxysm of lunacy who broke a quantity of windows and did other damage, there being no straitwaistcoat or other means of prevention of similar accidents'. In 1897 therefore, pay was increased to £33 a year for charge nurses, including the perk of 'beer-money', and a nursing home was built in 1898 with thirty-one bedrooms, sitting rooms and a dining room.

Medical treatments at this time appeared to involve a lot of beer and wine. Nursing mothers were prescribed a pint of beer a day, and port was regularly administered well into the 1900s.

This is a paediatric ward in Kingston hospital in 1920, looking somewhat spartan in contrast to today's wards packed with every conceivable kind of

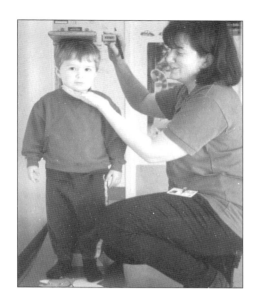

toy and staffed by play specialists. Here my son Christopher is measured in the Paediatric Outpatient Department by RSCN/RSGN Celia Richings, who is also the Children's Outpatient Coordinator.

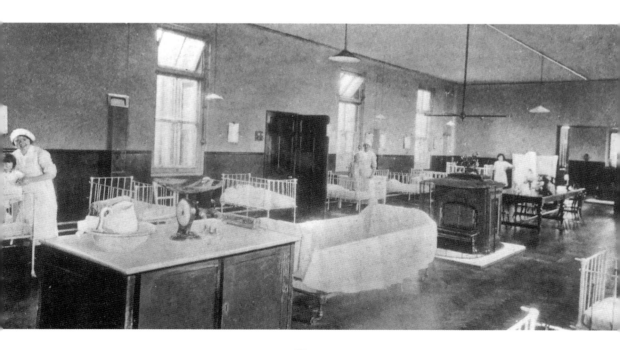

The hospital ran on voluntary contributions until the Government announced plans to convert it into a gynaecology department attached to Kingston hospital, after the birth of the NHS in 1948. A protest petition attracted the signatures of 20,000 people and doctors mounted guard on the building, even barricading themselves in, but in 1951 the cause was lost. In 1955 however funds raised allowed the purchase of Coombe Manor, costing £10,000 plus £19,000 for work and equipment. This New Victoria Hospital opened in 1958 and has since treated over half a million patients. It is one of the country's foremost private hospitals but retains charitable status and profits are re-invested in the hospital.

The Victoria Hospital was built to commemorate Queen Victoria's Diamond Jubilee, and was in fact Kingston's first general hospital. It was opened in 1898 by the Duke of Cambridge, who donated the three-acre site opposite the workhouse. The

The old photograph was taken in 1898 at the opening of the original Victoria Hospital. Today a welcoming face greets visitors and patients arriving in reception.

The Cleaves Almshouses in 1897 are still used for the same purpose today and are almost identical, bar the modern cars parked outside. In the early years Kingston's multitude of charities provided education and grants for the poor, but sadly were taken advantage of by many down-and-outs, and tricksters. By the 1860s there would be a 'cursing, fighting, disorderly mob' with 'scenes shocking to witness' when handouts took place, and this led town Alderman Frederick Gould to campaign for reform. This success resulted in eight of the charities pooling resources for education.

The other charities merged in 1874, except for one. William Cleave died in 1665, leaving money in his will 'for the erecting and building of a convenient house for six poor men and six poor women of honest life and reputation'. Cleaves Almshouses were built in 1669, in London Road, and are today administered by the Kingston United Charities.

The South Western Sanitary Laundry, L

" We are leaving Twickenham, and if ever I live in this district again, shall always send to your laundry, as the work has always been most satisfactory."

The South Western Sanitary Laundry was situated in Oil Mill Lane, pictured here in 1909. The horses and carts are lined up ready to collect or deliver laundry from and to the people of Kingston, a wonderful image sadly reaching its demise in 1937. By this time, the rise of the domestic washing-machine had led to the closure of many laundries. Oil Mill Lane is now Villiers Road and the site of the laundry is covered by a new housing estate on Winery Road and surrounding streets. In 1914 the laundry had a temporary minor crisis when all of its horses were commandeered by the Army.

Washdaze is a launderette and dry cleaners on Kings Road, possessing no horses but offering a service wash with a smile, thanks to Betty, here in the doorway complete with Ariel.

This irresistible photograph shows pupils at Bonner Hill School in 1908. The children are engrossed in making models out of plasticine, while the walls and window sill are adorned with pictures of all kinds and flowers. Bonner Hill was the first school to be launched after the Balfour Act of 1902, which enabled Kingston to administer its own elementary schools. It was opened in Villiers Road in 1906, with buildings and teaching methods well ahead of their time. In 1980, Bonner Hill merged with Rivermead and became Tudor School, which in turn

Chapter 7

PLACES OF LEARNING

closed in 1986. The original school was demolished in 1983 and housing has now been built where it once stood.

In 1561, Queen Elizabeth founded Kingston's famous grammar school here, fourteen years after it ceased to be used as a chapel. For over 300 years it was the centre of the school's life, known as the 'Big Schoolroom' until a government inspection in 1865 stated it to be 'singularly ill-adapted for educational purposes' and far too small for the fifty-two pupils attending. A new school was built across the road and opened in 1878.

The Lovekyn chapel has remained in use as part of the school premises ever since, including as a gymnasium from 1904-1936 and the woodwork centre from 1980-1992. An appeal then raised £150,000 to fully restore the chapel, which has since been used for music and the arts by both the school and the community. The restoration was formally recognised by the visit of HRH Princess Alexandra on 27 April 2000.

Lovekyn chapel in London Road was originally a chantry chapel called St Mary Magdalene, founded in 1309 by John Lovekyn. It is the one remaining free-standing chantry chapel in England and since 1927 has been a starred Grade II listed building. It is also the oldest complete building in Kingston.

In 1904 the Kingston Endowed School's Governors changed the name from Queen Elizabeth's School to Kingston Grammar School, as it has remained ever since. The present site on the London Road now stretches back to the Fairfield, representing phases in the school's development. The London Road frontage dates from 1878, the Assembly Hall linking this to the Lower School was built in the 1920s, while the library, seminar room and Art and Technology Centre were built in the 1990s. In 1926 the school accepted direct grant status but reverted to full independence in 1976 as a day school for boys and girls between the ages of ten and nineteen.

The 1935 photograph is of pupils celebrating George V's Silver Jubilee. They are dressed in Elizabethan costume and are riding on a replica Lovekyn chapel in a procession of floats passing through Kingston town centre. Today's pupils are working in the school's Information and Communication Technology Centre; computers throughout the school are networked and all pupils have their own e-mail address.

This building was the first of the Tiffin Schools, built on Kingston's Fairfield. It is pictured here in 1880 shortly after opening, together with four of its pupils, clearly budding cricketers. Tiffin Schools came into being after the merging of income from eight local charities, including those of brothers Thomas and John Tiffin, wealthy seventeenth-century brewers, who left money to educate and clothe needy Kingston children. The funds were put towards the grammar school's new building, and were used to create two new 'lower middle class schools' for boys and girls, to be known as Tiffin Schools.

Today the original Tiffin building is still a school, the home of St Joseph's Roman Catholic Primary School. The building has changed little, but the trees show the passage of time.

There were separate sections in the new Tiffin School, for 150 girls and 150 boys, and the fees were £3 a year per child, compared to £10 10s at the grammar school.

Very quickly the new school became overcrowded, and an eighteenth-century mansion called Elmfield in London Road was bought, and a new school built in its grounds. This opened in 1929 and flourishes today. Tiffin School joins the grammar school as being among the highest academic achievers in the United Kingdom.

Pupils from both 1921 and today are photographed in Canbury Gardens, but how different they look. In 1921 the boys are clearly enjoying dressing up as marauding Saxon warriors as part of the Kingston Church Pageant,

chasing after some demure-looking maidens. Today they are finishing an energetic Saturday morning's rowing at the Kingston Rowing Club headquarters.

This was the scene at Tiffin Girls' School in 1941. These large trenches were built in front of the school and were recently rediscovered when the new Fern Hill Primary School car-park was being laid out, Fern Hill being to the right but not in the photograph. Tiffin Girls moved next-door, to the left, in 1980, into the building which had previously been occupied by Tudor School, created by merging Bonner Hill with Rivermead.

The old Tiffin Girls' School is now the North Kingston Centre, home of adult education classes, and Kingston Local History Room among others. The Local History Room opened in 1992, when Kingston Museum was refurbished. Mayor and Mayoress Edwards attended the opening, as did the Heritage Officer, Anne McCormack.

Children have always loved learning by dressing up. The wonderful photograph below taken at Bonner Hill School in 1922 shows girls and boys celebrating Empire Day with banners and costumes representing countries far and wide.

Today, pupils from St John's Primary School visit Kingston Museum for a history lesson, dressing up in the Victorian costumes of a gentleman and lady, with her lady-in-waiting in attendance. St John's School is in Portland Road, opened in 1871 by the Revd Arnold Letchworth, curate of St John's, when he offered a prayer and gave an address to the children and parents. In 1886 there were 85 pupils in 'accommodation for 100 children at the government requirement of eight square foot for each child'. Today the school has grown to accommodate 270 three to eleven year olds.

The opening ceremony of Kingston Free Public Library, in May 1903. The mayor is Thomas Lyne. On the mayoress's left is Andrew Carnegie who helped pay for the library and who officially opened the premises now almost 100 years ago. Today the staff appear much more informal and relaxed on the doorstep and are extremely helpful inside. The library manager here is Sue Hurlock.

In the 1940s Kingston was given a gift of a travelling library from the *Whig-Standard* newspaper of Kingston, Canada. It had a capacity of 1,400 volumes and visited Tudor Drive, which now has its own library, and the junction of Cardinal and Hollybush Roads. It had to be towed to these sites by a commercially hired lorry at 10s 6d a time.

Kingston Museum was built in 1904 as an adjunct of the public library, designed by Alfred Cox in English Renaissance style. Both are pictured here in the 1930s. In 1992 the museum closed for a £300,000 refurbishment including cleaning of the brickwork, replacing the heating system and fencing, and most importantly replacement of the belvedere on the roof. The original had been removed possibly in the 1960s as it was dangerous, so the new one was built, with the help of photographs, to resemble the old design.

The museum re-opened in 1993 with a modernised art gallery and permanent displays showing the history of Kingston to Saxon times. Thanks to a National Lottery grant of nearly £105,000 the transformation was completed in 1997 with the opening of 'Town of Kings', a magnificent display taking Kingston's history to the present day.

The Fairfield was enclosed and saved as a public space by Major John Williams in 1865. He held office three times over, and this was one of his memorable moves for Kingston. Several market functions were transferred from the Market Place, including the cattle fair, seen here in 1907 from one of the library windows. The horse fair moved here in 1866 from the area north of All Saints known as the Horsefair; the road there still has the name today. Since then, many public events and occasions have taken place on the Fairfield; the Kingston Tudor Pageant in 1917, King George V's Jubilee in 1935 and the exciting arrival by helicopter of Eddie Calvert in 1955, bringing his 'Golden Trumpet' to play at the Regal to name a few.

The modern view is also from the library, the gates of which have not changed. Part of the Fairfield is now owned by the grammar school and used by pupils for sports training and events. The trees have grown obscuring the view but the Fairfield is still an open space for the enjoyment of the people of Kingston.

A Thomas Tilling horse bus stands outside the Druids Head Inn, in Kingston Market Place, around 1912, about to leave for Richmond. Until then, Kingston's fortunes had been closely linked to the long haul coaches, as more than twenty services used the town as a first stop on journeys to the south and west. Travelling by coach, however, required booking in advance, usually in pubs, and the new horse omnibuses did away with this. They also followed timetables greatly reducing travel times, and omnibus companies soon began competing fiercely for custom.

Chapter 8

TRANSPORT

There were constant reports of serious assaults between drivers, or of vehicles racing to try and run one another off the road.

The 1870 Tramways Act paved the way for vast expansion of horse trams in London, but they never reached Kingston. Instead, the electric tram quickly took over. There was much dispute about who should run the development scheme; some favoured London United Tramways whose chairman, Sir Clifton Robinson, lived in Hampton, while others felt Kingston Council should have the say over demolition of buildings and widening of roads in the Borough. An election in 1900 voted in favour of the LUT.

On 3 April 1905 the mayor of Kingston took a pickaxe to the first stone, and the mammoth task of laying thirty-two miles of tramlines serving Kingston, Surbiton and New Malden had begun. A hundred men were involved in the largest project of its kind to date in Britain, and the cost was around a million pounds. The *Surrey Comet* told of 'many quaint buildings, cherished memories of a bygone age' being demolished for the widening of roads, and 'complete chaos on almost every hand'.

The 1905 photograph shows just such work taking place on London Road, looking west towards the river. Today there is no trace of the tramlines, and the double-decker bus is a more familiar sight.

At midnight on 11 February 1906, Sir Clifton Robinson drove a tram over Kingston bridge on a trial run of the new service. The official launch took place on 1 March 1906, seen here amid the cheering crowds as a procession of three trams crossed Kingston bridge, through Clarence Street and London Road, and up Kingston Hill to the terminus at the George and Dragon pub. The mayor, Alderman Henry Minnitt, drove the first tram, although closely supervised by the chief driver, Lewis Bruce. A celebration lunch took place at Nuthalls Restaurant afterwards.

Trams were replaced by trolleybuses from 1931, again run by the LUT. In Kingston the service began on 15 June that year. However, they were not to last long; in 1954 with the advent of cheaper and cleaner diesel fuel, it was announced that they would be phased out. The last London trolleybus ran in May 1968, since when the motorbus has reigned supreme.

In 1834, Parliament authorised a London to Southampton railway line. Originally, largely due to local opposition, there was no central Kingston station but one in Surbiton instead. The first Kingston station was therefore little more than a hut to the west of the present day Ewell Bridge Road. The social and economic life in Kingston and the surrounding areas began to change; land value rose, new roads and houses were built and the population soared. Between 1841 and 1861, following the advent of the railway, numbers doubled from eight to sixteen thousand. With no central station, Kingston's trade began to suffer. In May 1861 work began to bring a branch line from Twickenham to Kingston via Hampton Wick.

Before the railway, Fife Road and all the land south of Canbury Lane to Clarence Street were covered by market gardens; in the event, Kingston Station itself was built on the site of one of the largest tithe barns in Britain. It has changed completely since the old photograh was taken at the turn of the nineteenth century.

In 1912 Thomas Octave Murdoch (TOM) Sopwith founded his Sopwith Aviation Company in what used to be Kingston's roller skating rink, at No. 1 Canbury Park Road. His workforce was initially 7, but due to the First World War had risen to 3,500 only 5 years later. Sopwith's first Kingston aeroplane was the Tabloid, capable of 90mph, the fastest plan at the time and the first of the single-seat aircraft used in the First World War.

On 1 June 1918 the first plane at the new factory in Richmond Road was finished. It wasn't long before Sopwith was producing 90 planes a week, mainly Snipes and Salamanders, the latter seen here in production that year. Following the war Sopwith Aviation closed on 15 November 1920, but was replaced on the same day by H.G. Hawker Engineering, named after Harry Hawker, Sopwith's

young test pilot who tragically died flying only the following year.

Aircraft production at the site ended in 1992 with the closure of what had become British Aerospace. More than 44,000 aircraft had been produced and there had never been an aerial campaign involving the UK without a Kingston aircraft flying. New housing estates cover the site today.

Famous names from motoring history have lived in Kingston; Herbert Austin who built the Austin 7 in 1923, Captain Archie Frazer Nash, the sports car pioneer, Kenelm Lee Guinness, Sir Malcolm Campbell and Henry Segrave, who in turn set world land speed records, lived on Kingston Hill in the 1920s and '30s. At the same time the Leyland Motor Company was making the Trojan car in Kingston at the factory which became British Aerospace.

Here the traffic is building up on Clarence Street in 1963, only the year after it became a one-way street to ease congestion. Today, however, several huge multi-storey car parks such as this one of Bentalls, are needed throughout Kingston to accommodate all the vehicles of many thousands of visitors and shoppers.

Cars first appeared in Kingston's streets in 1902. In 1903 the *Surrey Comet* reported the first local accident, in which a speeding car had swerved and braked to avoid a horse-drawn vehicle, and ended up on the pavement crashed into the window of Mr Peter Jamieson's bakery shop.

It had been hoped that the advent of the motor car would ease congestion, it being smaller and faster than horse-drawn vehicles. However, this was not the case. In 1913 a vehicle count in Portsmouth Road took place, and only 12 years later the same census showed a 125 per cent increase.

This led to the building of the bypass. In 1927 the Kingston Bypass was officially opened by Prime Minister Stanley Baldwin, making history as the first modern bypass road in Britain. The photograph below was taken from New Malden in 1957. Today the A3 has been modernised and widened, and the volume of traffic has increased somewhat from the early days.

Richmond Park is currently the subject of debate regarding it being a through route for traffic. Proposals are being considered to close the park to vehicles, amid opposition from local residents. Above is Kingston Gate in 1904, at the junction of what are now Kings and Queens Roads in North Kingston. When the park was first opened to the public, ladders were used for pedestrian access over the enclosing walls. The park gates were only used for coaches and were otherwise kept closed in order to prevent the deer from escaping.

The gates have been closed recently during the foot and mouth outbreak but have now re-opened, thankfully, once again allowing some escape into its peaceful green woodlands and meadows, away from the bustle of daily life.